YELLOWSTONE

WILD AND WONDER JOURNAL

THERMAL PATTERN AT GRAND PRISMATIC SPRING

BLUE FUNNEL SPRING, WEST THUMB GEYSER BASIN

> "The preservation idea, born in Yellowstone, spread around
> the world. Scores of nations have preserved areas of natural
> beauty and historical worth so that all mankind will have the
> opportunity to reflect on their natural and cultural heritage,
> and to return to nature and be spiritually reborn in it. Of
> all the benefits from Yellowstone National Park, this may
> be the greatest."

— National Park Service

THERMAL STEAM NEAR MOUNT WASHBURN

SAWMILL GEYSER, UPPER GEYSER BASIN

LOWER FALLS & THE GRAND CANYON OF THE YELLOWSTONE RIVER

YELLOWSTONE LAKE

"No other lake in North America of equal area lies so high as the Yellowstone, or gives birth to so noble a river.... In calm weather it is a magnificent mirror for the woods and mountains and sky, now pattered with hail and rain, now roughened with sudden storms that send waves to fringe the shores and wash its border of gravel and sand."

—John Muir

CINNAMON BLACK BEAR

BISON CROSSING THE YELLOWSTONE RIVER

MOOSE FALLS

GRAND PRISMATIC SPRING, MIDWAY GEYSER BASIN

> *"Mute with astonishment, we gazed upon this expanse of steaming,
> sapphire-colored water so surpassingly transparent that the thousand
> fantastical forms on the festooned walls could be distinguished under
> the crystal liquid."*

—Jules Leclercq

ELK AT SWAN LAKE FLATS

RED FOX SLEEPING IN WINTER

ASPENS IN WINTER, LAMAR VALLEY

"BOBBYSOCK TREES" IN THE LOWER GEYSER BASIN

"The forces that created earth are constantly with us, altering landscapes over time. In the future, Yellowstone may again be buried under ice, ash, or water. In man's geologic nanosecond of existence, however, it is fortunate we have the present version to learn from and wonder at."

—Pete Bengeyfield

BALD EAGLE, YELLOWSTONE LAKE

SAPPHIRE POOL, BISCUIT BASIN

THERMAL PATTERN IN THE UPPER GEYSER BASIN

THERMAL PATTERN IN THE NORRIS GEYSER BASIN

"The geysers, the extraordinary hot springs, the lakes, the mountains, the canyon and cataracts unite to make this region something not paralleled elsewhere on the globe."

—President Theodore Roosevelt

OLD FAITHFUL GEYSER, UPPER GEYSER BASIN

ASPEN LEAVES IN FALL

FALL ALONG SODA BUTTE CREEK

BISON NEAR MAMMOTH HOT SPRINGS

"Perhaps no animal in the history of any nation has ever played a more important role than the American bison."

—David A. Dary

ELK IN THE NORTHERN RANGE

SUMMIT OF MT. WASHBURN

LOWER FALLS OF THE YELLOWSTONE RIVER

ELECTRIC PEAK

"We must preserve parks not only for all the things that they can do for us today, but for values and services they hold that we have not yet had the wisdom to recognize."

—Paul Schullery

BULL ELK ALONG THE MADISON RIVER

BIGHORN SHEEP IN WINTER

ORANGE SPRING MOUND, MAMMOTH HOT SPRINGS

THE LAMAR RIVER MEANDERING THROUGH LAMAR VALLEY

"There is something in the wild romantic scenery of this valley which I cannot...describe; but the impressions made upon my mind while gazing from a high eminence on the surrounding landscape...can never efface from my memory....For my own part, I almost wished I could spend the remainder of my days in a place like this where happiness and contentment seemed to reign in wild romantic splendor."

—Osborne Russell

OLD FAITHFUL GEYSER UNDER THE MILKY WAY

RAVEN

UNDINE FALLS IN WINTER

GRIZZLY BEAR

"To those of us who enter the Yellowstone wilderness, who take the chance of a bear encounter, who experience Yellowstone first hand, many rich rewards may come our way. We may get to watch a wild creature go about its day, aware of our presence but otherwise heedless of our existence.... We may feel the earth shake under our feet...or feel the call of the wild when a wolf pack howls.... Whatever the reward, we come to realize that Yellowstone and other wild places are not the exception, but rather the authentic, the original, the real."

—Michael J. Yochim

TROUT CREEK, HAYDEN VALLEY

RIVERBEND
PUBLISHING

An imprint of Globe Pequot, the trade division of The Rowman & Littlefield Publishing Group, Inc.

4501 Forbes Blvd., Ste. 200
Lanham, MD 20706

www.rowman.com

Distributed by NATIONAL BOOK NETWORK

Yellowstone: Wild and Wonder Journal
© 2024 Christopher Cauble
caublephotography.com

ISBN: 978-1-60639-142-6

Printed and bound in India

Cover and layout design by Sarah Cauble
sarahcauble.com

Quote attributions in order of appearance:

National Park Service, Yellowstone: "*The Place Where Hell Bubbled Up*," A History of the First National Park
John Muir, "The Yellowstone National Park," *The Atlantic*, April 1898
Jules Leclercq, *Yellowstone, Land of Wonders: Promenade in North America's National Park*, 1883
Pete Bengeyfield, *Incredible Vision: The Wildlands of Greater Yellowstone*
President Theodore Roosevelt
David A. Dary, *The Buffalo Book*
Paul Schullery, Aubrey Haines Lecture, Yellowstone National Park, 2012
Osborne Russell, fur trapper, 1839
Michael J. Yochim, *Essential Yellowstone: A Landscape of Memory and Wonder*